CHUPACABRA

ARE THEY REAL?

CREATIVE EDUCATION · CREATIVE PAPERBACKS

Published by Creative Education and Creative Paperbacks

P.O. Box 227, Mankato, Minnesota 56002

Creative Education and Creative Paperbacks are imprints of The Creative Company

www.thecreativecompany.us

Design and production by **Christine Vanderbeek**

Art direction by **Rita Marshall**

Printed in the United States of America

Photographs by Alamy (FILM STILLS, Adrian Grabowski, Peter Tsai Photography), Corbis (Annette Fournet, Jason Langer/ Glasshouse Images), Dreamstime (Hermann Danzmayr), Getty Images (Chris Ward, Todd Warnock, WIN-Initiative), Science Source (Jaime Chirinos), Shutterstock (Alexlky, andreiuc88, Balazs Kovacs Images, bastetamon, Zacarias Pereira da Mata, fotozotti, Kjpargeter, Kletr, rudall30)

Library of Congress Cataloging-in-Publication Data

Murray, Laura K.   Chupacabra / Laura K. Murray.   p. cm. – (Are they real?)   Includes index.   Summary: A high-interest inquiry into the possible existence of North America's fabled blood-sucking chupacabras, emphasizing reported sightings and seekers as well as strange findings.

ISBN 978-1-60818-762-1 (hardcover)   **ISBN 978-1-62832-370-2** (pbk)   **ISBN 978-1-56660-804-6** (ebook)

This title has been submitted for CIP processing under LCCN 2016008262.

CCSS: RI.1.1, 2, 4, 5, 6, 7, 10; RI.2.1, 2, 4, 5, 6, 7; RI.3.1, 2, 5, 6, 7; RF.1.1, 2, 3, 4; RF.2.3, 4; RF.3.3, 4

First Edition HC 9 8 7 6 5 4 3 2 1   **First Edition PBK** 9 8 7 6 5 4 3 2 1

CONTENTS

A NOISE

A farmer named Jorge Talavera waits in the dark. He is guarding his animals. What was that loud noise? Jorge sees something with sharp, red teeth!

ITS EYES ARE GLOWING!

WILD BEAST

People talk about the chupacabra as a wild beast. They say it drinks animal blood. Its name means "goat sucker" in Spanish. It may live in **LATIN AMERICA** or the southern United States.

WHAT DOES THE CHUPACABRA LOOK LIKE?

The chupacabra could be four to five feet (1.2–1.5 m) tall. It runs and jumps on two legs. It has sharp claws and fangs. It may have spikes or wings on its back! Its eyes glow in the dark.

WHAT DOES THE CHUPACABRA DO?

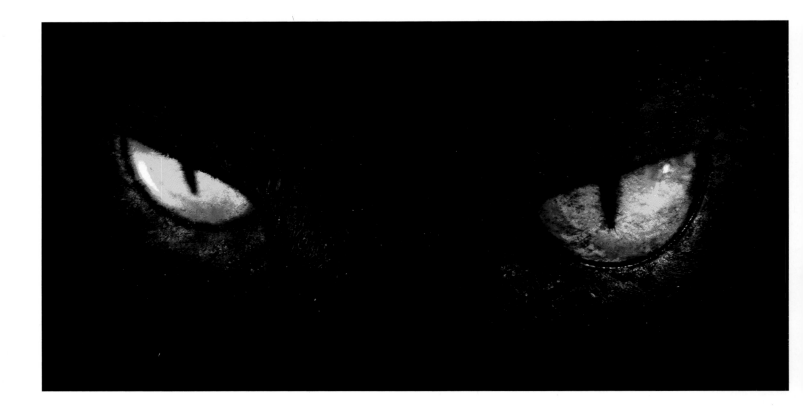

The chupacabra acts like a **VAMPIRE**. It bites the necks of some animals. It may stun **PREY** with its eyes. But it has not hurt people.

Sometimes people find strange animals. Could they be chupacabras? **ZOOLOGISTS** usually say they are some type of dog. Other times it is a **MYSTERY**!

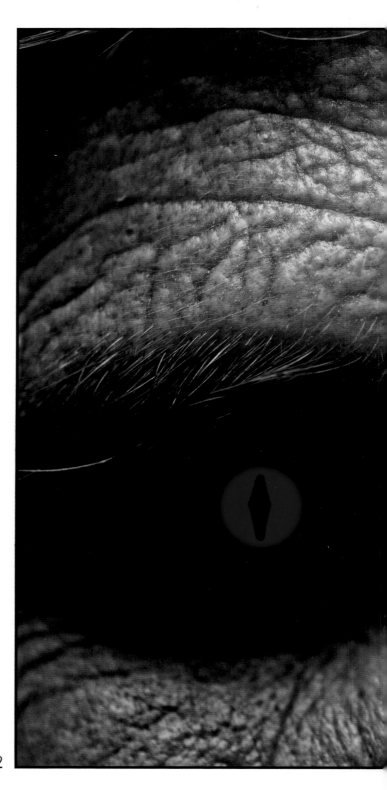

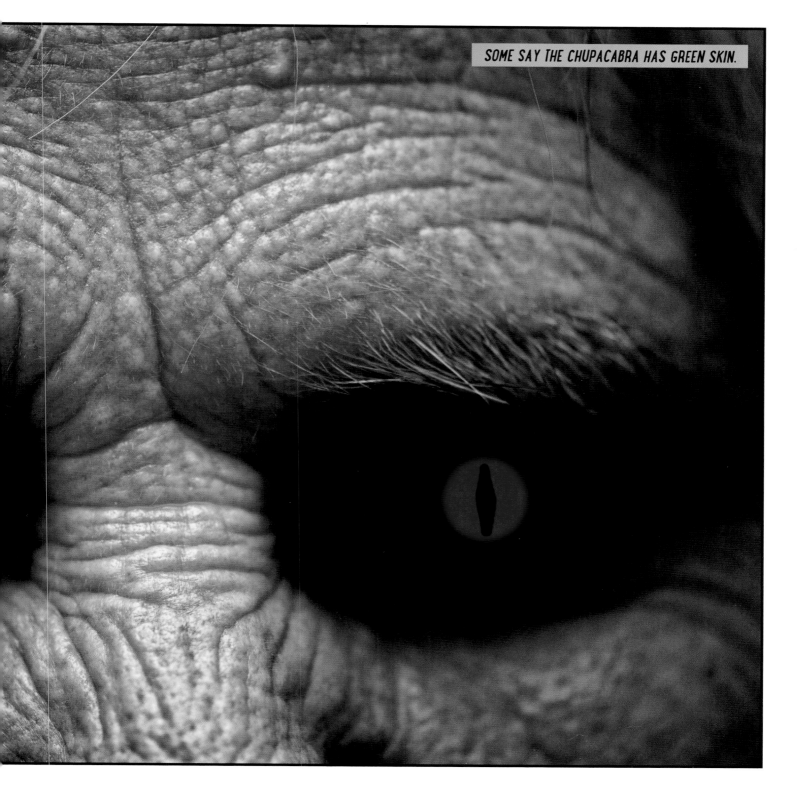

SOME SAY THE CHUPACABRA HAS GREEN SKIN.

STORIES OF THE
CHUPACABRA

In 1995, Madelyn Tolentino said she saw a monster in Puerto Rico. It left behind slime.

Did she see a chupacabra? Or did she make it up?

You can find the chupacabra in movies, video games, and more.

Chupacabra is a book by Roland Smith. A chupacabra shows up in Fantastic Four comic books, too.

CHUPACABRA ENCOUNTERS

A writer named Benjamin Radford looked for the chupacabra. He talked to people around the world. He does not think the chupacabra is real. Maybe it is just a **LEGEND**.

What would you do if
you saw a chupacabra?

HISS AND
YELL TO SCARE
IT AWAY!

INVESTIGATE IT!
THE MAKING OF A MONSTER

Create your own monster! You will need paper and coloring supplies. Think about where your monster lives. What does it eat? Does it have special powers? Is it scary or friendly? Give your monster a name.

WHAT DOES YOUR MONSTER LOOK LIKE?

GLOSSARY

LATIN AMERICA Mexico, Central America, South America, and the Caribbean islands

LEGEND a well-known story that may not be true

MYSTERY something that is hard to understand

PREY animals that are eaten by other animals

VAMPIRE a monster that sucks blood

ZOOLOGIST a person who studies animals

WEBSITES

Mexico

http://kids.nationalgeographic.com/explore/countries/mexico

Learn more about Mexico, one possible home of the chupacabra.

Monster Coloring Pages

http://www.coloring.ws/monsters.htm

Find a famous monster to print and color.

Note: Every effort has been made to ensure that the websites listed above are suitable for children, that they have educational value, and that they contain no inappropriate material. However, because of the nature of the Internet, it is impossible to guarantee that these sites will remain active indefinitely or that their contents will not be altered.

READ MORE

Peterson, Megan Cooley. *Encountering the Chupacabra and Other Cryptids*. North Mankato, Minn.: Capstone, 2014.

Townsend, John. *Strange Creatures*. Mankato, Minn.: Smart Apple Media, 2010.

INDEX